Come Back to Your Senses

From Burnout to Sustainable Self-Care

Come Back to Your Senses

From Burnout to Sustainable Self-Care

By Barbara Lynn Voss, MA, MFT

Barbara Lynn Voss, Publisher

Copyright 2009 Barbara Lynn Voss

Edited by Janis Tidwell

Copyedited by Priscilla Stuckey

Cover Design and Illustration by Barbara Lynn Voss

Graphic Art Illustrations by Frederick Dowd

Photographs by Frederick Dowd and Barbara Lynn Voss

Photograph of Author by Marie Gregorio-Oviedo

Second paperback printing, December 2009

ISBN: 978-0-578-04408-8

This book is dedicated to my mom and dad, who taught me how to take my first small steps.

Contents

Acknowledgments

I want to thank my husband, Frederick Dowd, for his practical support, loving-kindness, and sense of humor throughout the process of writing and publishing this book.

I want to thank Christina K. Bjornstedt, MA, for her heartfelt support, loving wisdom, and unrelenting kindness as I took my small steps of personal growth.

I want to thank Priscilla Stuckey, PhD, for the doors she opened for me and her kind, loving support over many years as we've grown in our appreciation for all living beings.

I want to thank Janis Tidwell for her loving thoughtfulness, inspiring conversations, and insightful editorial comments throughout the process of developing this book.

Thank you. This book is possible because of all of you.

Preface

If you feel burned out or on your way to burning out, this book is for you. Burnout is a slow wearing away of your emotional, physical, mental, spiritual, and living-space health. Burnout takes time to manifest and may take some time to recover.

Recovering from burnout is typically a slow process of building a sustainable path of nurturing your emotions, body, mind, and spirit as well as your connection to others and your environment. Recovering from burnout is a process to begin one step at a time. This book is a starting place to guide you to care for yourself step-by-step.

When you're burned out, your nerves are shot. You're so tired that you don't feel much at all. You may not even remember how to feel, think, or be connected to others. You can't feel your dreams or feel much of anything; you've gone flat.

This book is designed to help you discover ways to care for yourself that are sustainable for you. Many books describe elaborate steps for self-care, whereas this book focuses on you discovering through your experience, not through an intellectual exercise, what works for you.

The suggestions in this book are meant to slow you down and give you time to nurture yourself. Self-care that is appropriate for you emerges from your own experiences, not from those of the people around you. It may seem that the process is slow. Nevertheless, the accumulated effect of each step builds a foundation for your sustainable self-care.

This book does not address head-on the typical causes of burnout, such as job or career challenges, financial stress, marital stress, loss of dreams, or long-term health care issues. Rather, the purpose of this book is to provide you with self-support so that you eventually can face any changes you may want to make with more focus, energy, and self-compassion.

You need to do simple acts of self-care to soothe yourself in order to know how to approach the bigger issues. For now, put those bigger issues on the shelf and attend to your own daily life.

This book is meant to be carried with you to remind you to take care of yourself. You can use the space at the bottom of each page to make notes to yourself.

Each week offers a suggested practice that you can experience and continue developing during and after the process. To discover sustainable self-care rather than one-time events that fizzle out, you need to find small incremental changes that are nurturing for you. Then, you can develop the habit of repeating what is nurturing for you. This book helps you explore little steps that you may want to integrate into your life in order to recover from burnout.

Introduction

I experienced burnout due to a combination of factors. I was holding down two jobs, breaking up a significant relationship, experiencing financial stress, and having a long-term medical issue, which was diagnosed correctly only after persistently asking the medical community for answers. I realized I had to find a way to stop focusing on the expectations of other people, stop some of my behaviors, and begin to center on myself and my own needs.

As I went through my own journey of healing my burnout, I learned to focus on small immediate steps I could take. In a way, it didn't matter how I felt about the steps, but it mattered that I took the steps. Each day the accumulated effect of small acts of care and kindness toward myself allowed me to rebuild a sense of joy, happiness, and peace in my life. I hope this book supports you on your own journey of growing in self-care. In being kind toward yourself, I hope you find your own sense of joy and peace, and a life of harmony.

Chapter One: Seeing Self-Care

Week 1: Gifts

Find a birthday card or a thank-you note you've received from a friend or family member. Choose a comfortable chair, sit down, and read it again. Look at the card and the message, and soak in the care your friend took in sending you this card.

If the cards are difficult to find, look around your house for a gift from a friend or family member. Hold the gift in your hands. Look at its texture. Remember the warmth and love that accompanied the gift.

If you can find a different card or gift for each day this week, take the time (it can be only 5 minutes) to pause and look at a heart-centered communication from a friend or family member. Remember the feeling of love and care that came with this card or gift.

Week 2: Plants

In your weekly trip to the grocery store, buy some fresh fruit, fresh vegetables, or a houseplant. Before you eat the fruit or vegetables, sit down (even for 2 minutes), and look at the colors in the fruits or vegetables. If you choose to look at a houseplant, sit down and look at the colors in the leaves, stem, or flowers.

As you look at these live fruits, vegetables, and plants, what do you notice about the colors? What do you notice about the shapes? What do you notice about the color hues and tones as the light changes during the day? Is there one type of fruit, vegetable, or houseplant you find especially beautiful?

Week 3: Faces

In a photo, look at a face of someone you love—your spouse, a child, brother, sister, parent, grandparent, aunt, uncle, cousin, or friend.

As you look at the person in a photo, notice the color of the eyes, the shape of the nose and mouth, the texture of the hair, the expression of the face and body. See the person.

In the space below, you might want to note: What is it you love about this person? What qualities in this person do you feel grateful for? What actions from this person do you feel grateful for? Each day this week, select a different person to see.

Week 4: Art at Home

Discover art in your home. For 5 minutes each day, look at paintings, photographs, sculptures, candles, jewelry, or objects in your house that you have there simply for the sake of beauty.

What is it you like about the art object you chose? What feelings, if any, does the object evoke in you? Is the object in the "right" place in your home for you to see and enjoy it? Is there another beautiful object you would like to add to your home environment, to enjoy seeing?

Week 5: Art in Your Community

Visit a local art museum, art gallery, or aquarium. Find a nice bench in front of your favorite art object or fish tank, and look at the painting or watch the fish swim. Take the time to look at the colors, shapes, lines, values of the art or the live art as they move. Is there any art or any fish that you are particularly drawn to, that you find particularly pleasing to look at?

A visit to a local art museum or aquarium may take some planning and may happen easily only on a weekend. However, you can often find small local art galleries on a neighborhood street, and you might visit them during your lunch break or drop by on your way home from work.

Taking even 15 to 30 minutes once or even a few times during this week to discover a source of beauty and relaxation can provide you with a sanctuary from the daily grind.

Week 6: The Drive

This week drive from work to home along a different route. Observe different buildings, landscapes, people, or activities.

If you can figure out multiple ways to drive either to work or from work, experiment with traveling on different roads. Was one route more scenic than another? Were drivers more rushed or polite on one route than another? Did you feel safer on one route than another? Did the time of day influence how much beauty you could see? Did you prefer one route over another going to work or coming home from work?

Week 7: TV

Limit the time you watch TV to an hour a day. Or, better yet, turn off the TV for one week. You can always record any program you wanted to watch this week.

Sometimes you may want to eliminate visual stimulation to enhance your sense of calm. Watching violent images over and over may upset you and add to your burnout. Also, watching TV passively might make you more tired, irritable, and sad, regardless of the images.

Alternatively, you can sit and spend the time in silence, take a walk, take a bath, paint a picture, or go to bed early. Give up TV for one week, and notice what you experience.

Chapter Two: Hearing Self-Care

Week 8: Music

Listen to soothing music of your choice for 15 minutes each day. Pick a time of day when you can relax and just listen. It could be before breakfast, at night right before bed, or on a break during the day using your headphones.

Notice any difference in your muscles, breathing, or attitudes after you listen to the music. How did you feel about the sound of calming music?

Week 9: Quiet

At some point during your workday, take a break for 15 minutes. Find a quiet conference room, or sit in your car, or go to a quiet church or park. If you work at home, leave your home office and sit in a quiet room in your house.

While you are sitting quietly, close your eyes and notice your breath. Count to 4 as you breathe in slowly. Hold your breath for a count of 4. Breathe out for 4 counts. Wait to breathe for 4 counts. Repeat the breathing process slowly again.

During the week you may be able to increase the count to 5 or 6. The purpose of this exercise is not to increase the numbers but to slow down and bring your attention to your breathing process. At the end of your break, you might want to acknowledge with gratitude your marvelous body and your life with each breath.

Week 10: Birds

Sit outside in your yard or at a park, and listen to the birds for 10 minutes. Close your eyes and listen to one bird singing, squawking, or calling. Can you hear different sounds from this one bird? Do any other birds respond to the songs or calls? When you open your eyes, can you find your feathered friend?

For fun, can you mimic the bird's call and say hello?

Week 11: Poems

Read a short poem, children's book, or nursery rhyme aloud to yourself. Choose a poem or passage that you like. It may be a story from your childhood or a poem with special meaning to you or a nursery rhyme you read to your children. Read it aloud, and notice the rhythm, the sound of the words, and the feelings you have after you've read it.

Although people typically read aloud to others, take the time each day to read to yourself, to read a writer's work you enjoy. Use the time to explore the sounds of the words, and play with them.

Read a storybook aloud to yourself or your children or someone else's children. Embellish the story, speaking as you think the characters would. Have fun!

Week 12: Singing

Select and play a favorite song each day, and sing along with the recording. Or sing your favorite song a cappella. Or sing a song with other people who also want to sing. You could sing in the car, the shower, around the house, or even on a walk.

What songs did you choose? Did they lead to other songs?

Week 13: Listen

When you are at work or at home in a relaxed setting where you do not have to be actively listening, instead of leaning forward to listen to people when they talk, sit or step back, and allow the sounds of people talking to come to you. Do not reach forward in your body, with your ears, or in your attention. Bring your attention to the back of your ears, and let the sounds of people talking come to you. Practice this for 5 minutes at a time during your workday or at home.

What did you notice?

Chapter Three: Smelling Self-Care

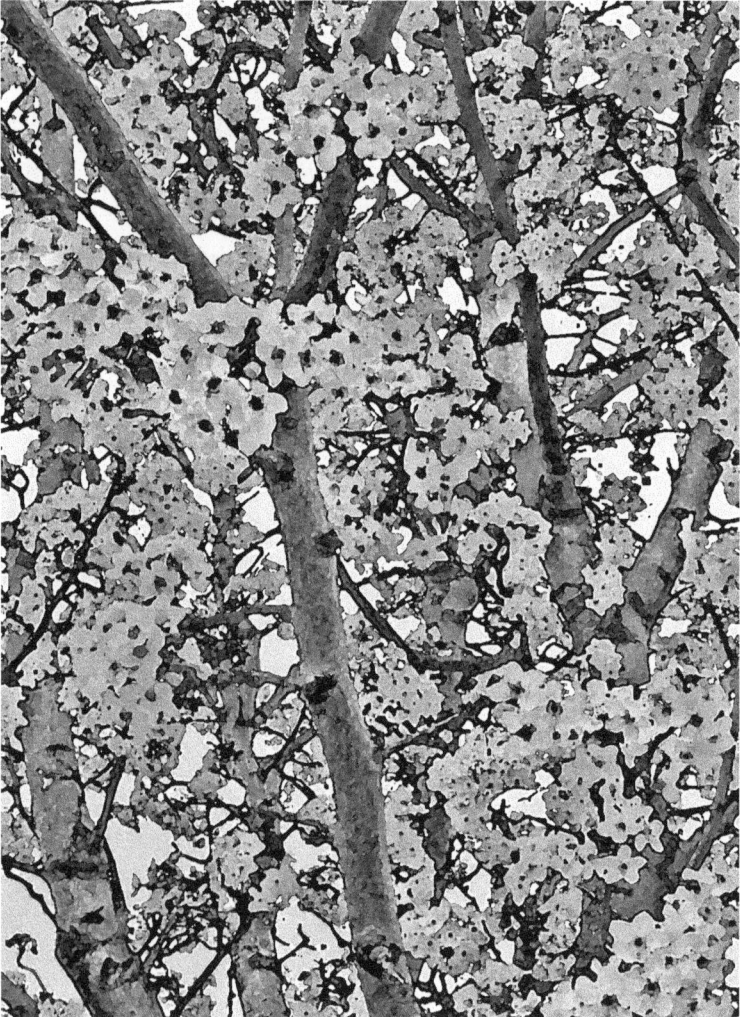

Week 14: Flowers

Pick, cut, or buy yourself some flowers with scents that please you. You may want to spend time in your garden, at a flower shop, at an arboretum, or in the woods to find the flowers that you enjoy. Place the flowers in a central area of your house, such as the kitchen table or your desk at home or work. Smell them every day. If you have more than one favorite type of flower, bring several into your environment.

What flowers do you love for their scent?

Week 15: Essential Oils

Essential oils can be used as scents in your environment to produce calming effects. Many grocery, bath and body, or gift stores carry aromatherapy essential oils. When you go to the store, smell the different scents and notice their effect on you. Do any of the scents evoke feelings of happiness or peace? You might want to purchase some oils. For many, the scents of lavender, rose, or cypress are calming.

During the week, take out your essential oil bottles, open them, and take a whiff. If you have an essential oil burner, use the burner as directed. You could also take a bath and pour some of the essential oil into your bathtub.

Release the wonderful scents into your home. What is your favorite scent? What scents allow you to relax?

Week 16: Fruits

When you shop at a grocery store this week, smell the fruit. Select your favorite fresh fruits, and sniff them. Pick up an apple or orange, a tray of strawberries, blueberries, or raspberries, and inhale deeply. Do you notice any difference in the brands? Do you notice any difference in the smell of the local fruits compared to the fruits shipped over long distances?

If you can, go to your local farmers' market. Smell the local fruit. Sniff the local vegetables, grains, honey, nuts, or herbs.

Do you notice any difference, for example, in the smell of a farmers' market fruit, like an apple, as compared to that of a grocery store local apple or a well-traveled apple?

What did you notice about the smells of the fruit? Were there any particular fruits you wanted to eat simply because of the smell? Were there any fruits you did not want to eat because of the smell?

Week 17: Spices

As you are cooking dinner this week, select one spice each evening from your cupboard to use for cooking. Take the time to sniff the cinnamon, turmeric, rosemary, sage, tarragon, or basil. Imagine what foods would taste even better with that one spice. Each day choose a different herb or spice that appeals to you to enhance your food.

Smell the food before you eat it. Did the spice bring out the smell of the food or overpower it? Did you like the smell of the spice after it was cooked? Did you discover any favorite spices this week?

Week 18: Air Filters

Even if you clean your bedroom meticulously, the air may still be dusty or moldy or have pet dander or chemical fumes from your mattress or odors from your room cleaners. Even if you get enough hours of sleep, you may not be getting the right quality of sleep, making you more exhausted during the day in spite of your best efforts. Although houseplants such as the gerbera daisy and bamboo palm serve as wonderful air filters by removing toxins from the air, air filters, particularly those with HEPA filters, allow you to breathe more easily and sleep more deeply.

You can purchase HEPA air filters for a single room, such as your bedroom. This may be a product to explore if you find you wake up in the morning more tired than when you went to bed.

If you decide to purchase a HEPA air filter, notice if you breathe easier at night. Do you notice if any smells around you are stronger or clearer because you are less congested and able to breathe easier?

Week 19: Cleaning Products

Many people, particularly children, are sensitive to chemicals, toxins, and pollution in their environment and could have undetected allergies. These allergies slowly weaken your body if they are triggered by chemicals continually present in your environment. This week, smell your cleaning products.

Each day target one group of products, such as cleaning products for dishes, laundry, floors, appliances, garage, car, garden, and yourself (your body, teeth, and hair). How do you feel when you sniff each of these products? Does your chest tighten up? Does your skin break out if you touch them? Do you feel weaker or stronger when you smell them? If you have trouble breathing near some products, you may need to throw them away and use plant-based or natural cleaners without harsh chemicals. Many cities provide places to dispose of household chemicals or pesticides so they don't get dumped into the environment.

You can experiment with any citrus fruit (lemons, oranges) as degreasers or plant-based oils (tea tree, eucalyptus) as disinfectants. A paste of baking soda and water is good for scouring. Diluted white vinegar is good for cleaning windows and killing bacteria, mold, and viruses. How do you feel when you smell these materials? How does your body respond when you smell these products?

Chapter Four: Tasting Self-Care

Week 20: Meals

For one meal a day, such as your dinner, take the time to eat slowly. Taste each spice, and savor each flavor added to the food. Place your spoon and fork down while you savor each bite of food. Pause. Pick up your utensils again, and eat. Silently thank the animals, plants, herbs, and water involved in providing your food.

Week 21: Favorite Foods Then and Now

Then: What was your favorite food that your parents cooked, baked, grilled, boiled, mixed, or made for you when you were a child? On your next shopping trip, buy the food or the ingredients for that food. Look up the recipe and make it. Then, eat your favorite food, savoring each bite.

Now: What is your favorite food that you like to cook, bake, grill, boil, mix, or make? On your next shopping trip, buy the food or the ingredients for that food. Look up the recipe and make it. Then, eat your favorite food, savoring each bite.

Did you taste something new about your favorite food? Is there a time of day you most like to eat your favorite food, or is anytime a good time for your favorite foods?

Week 22: Teatime

Many people prepare teas to drink as they socialize, bring comfort to another, or hold important conversations. The custom of tea drinking in order to become calm and gain perspective is prevalent throughout the world. On your next shopping trip, buy an assortment of herbal and green teas, and explore one each day.

Take time during your afternoon for a tea break. Go to your office kitchen or your home kitchen, and choose your tea for the day. Sit for 15 minutes slowly drinking your lemon tea, chamomile, blackberry, or green tea.

What taste appeals to you at teatime? What tea hits the spot? Does this tea evoke any memories? Would you like to share this teatime with one friend?

Week 23: Vegetable Soup

Vegetable soup is so soothing. What are your favorite vegetables? This week, make your favorite vegetable soup recipe. You can make enough soup for a week. Fill the soup with spices and vegetables you love. Take the time to enjoy one meal during the week eating slowly and in silence. Feel the soup begin to nurture you to your very core.

What are your favorite vegetables?

Week 24: Water

Pour a glass of water from your faucet. How does your water taste to you? Do you feel energized or drained after you drink the water? Water quality varies from neighborhood to neighborhood and may or may not taste good to you.

You might want to consider installing a water filter on your kitchen faucet to eliminate any bad tastes or extra chemicals in the water. Drinking tap water eliminates the need for bottled water. Often, if bottled water is heated or stored for long periods of time, phthalates, which are chemicals that disrupt hormones, are released into the water from the plastic. To carry your filtered water with you, you can also buy a steel, copper, or glass bottle. This not only saves you money but also provides a way for you to drink nourishing water.

What did you notice about the taste of different water?

Week 25: Foods to Eliminate

Some foods may be unhealthy for certain bodies because of allergies or differing body types or the food's effect on you. If you're struggling with feeling exhausted and burned out, it may be time to reduce or eliminate caffeine. Although caffeine supplies our bodies with an initial pick-me-up, over time it may wear down your adrenal glands, for example, leaving you more depleted.

This week, take the time to notice how you feel after you eat. Do you feel more or less energy? Do you feel energy briefly and then sink into a fog? You may need to experiment with eliminating foods from your diet and adding them in one at time to notice the effect of a particular food on your body. This may take more than a week. However, starting the process of noticing the effect of specific food on your body will help you know what is healthy for your body to eat.

Are there foods you already know you need to stop eating?

Chapter Five: Touching Self-Care

Week 26: Pets

Pet your pet. If you don't have a pet, borrow a friend's or neighbor's dog or cat to pet. Petting the fur of a cat or dog soothes both the humans and the animal. Even if it is only 5 minutes, spend some quality time each day this week brushing and petting your cat or dog.

Notice where on their bodies your animal friends like to be petted, scratched, or rubbed. Most animals provide instant feedback about this and will let you know.

If you have the energy, walk your dog or a friend's dog. Notice the bond you feel through the leash with the dog. Did you notice any emotional connection with your animal friend on your walk?

If you have the time and energy for a further adventure, visit a local animal shelter, such as a local Humane Society of the United States or ASPCA, and pet their dogs or cats.

How did you feel after this connection with an animal friend? What did you notice about your level of tiredness?

Week 27: Hugs

Hug your spouse, children, or friends this week. Pay attention as you hug your family members and closest friends. As you hug them, send each person your love and kindness. If you are not feeling particularly friendly toward someone, don't hug that person. Wait until you are able to touch and be hugged, and hug them in return.

After you hug someone, did you notice any shift in you or in the other person? Did you feel more relaxed or stressed? Did you feel calm or awkward? What feelings, if any, did this person draw out in you?

Week 28: Pens

This week take a trip to a gift store, drugstore, or art supply store to search for pens. Find the pen section of the store, and hold different pens. Feel the weight of them in the hand you use for writing. Write with each pen. Which pen feels best in your hand? Purchase a pen that fits your hand, and use it as your personal pen for you alone.

During the week, when you use your pen, notice the smoothness of it, how it fits to your hand, and any texture on the body of the pen.

Week 29: Soaps

Many bath, gift, or drugstores have a variety of soaps. This week discover the world of soaps. Buy a different scent or texture for each day this week. Some stores even give free soap samples. In your shower or bath, notice the different texture, scent, or feeling on your skin. What do you like? What scent feels the most relaxing to you? Is there a brand of soap that soothes you the best?

Week 30: Baths

Take time for a hot bath this week. Put a sign on the door: Do Not Disturb. Lock the bathroom door, and enjoy 30 minutes of time alone. Scent your hot bath with your new soaps or essential oils. Use Epsom salts to help you relax.

Feel the soap on your body. Do you like all the soaps equally well? Are some soaps too soapy, some too harsh, some too smelly? What feels relaxing on your body?

Week 31: Massage

For some people a massage is a new experience while for others it is a favorite event. This week schedule either a reflexology treatment or a massage. Reflexology treatments are foot massages that nourish your body through touching trigger points on the soles of your feet.

Find a reflexologist or massage therapist you trust. Choose someone who can be flexible and massage you as softly or firmly as you need this week.

How was the experience for you? How did you know you trusted the massage therapist or reflexologist?

Week 32: Stretching

Yoga may be a new experience for you, or perhaps you enjoy it regularly. In either case, this week find a beginning yoga class and an instructor who teaches restorative poses. If you are feeling tired and burned out, you do not need a physically demanding class. Check out yoga classes until you find a relaxing, restorative class.

Attend one class this week. Notice how you felt before you came into the class and after you left the class. Did you have more or less energy? Did you feel more or less relaxed? How did you feel with the teacher? Did you feel safe? Did your body feel healthier?

Chapter Six: Feeling Self-Care

Week 33: Sleep

Go to bed early. Every night this week, go to bed at least 30 minutes earlier than usual. Even if you can't fall asleep, lie in bed and relax.

You could do any or all of these exercises:

You might want to listen to relaxing music as you drift off to sleep.

Or you might want to notice where you are tense, tighten that muscle even more, and then relax the muscle.

Or you might want to progressively relax your body by tightening your feet and then relaxing them. Progress up your body, and continue to next tighten your calf muscles and relax them. Progress up your body and continue consecutively to tighten and relax your thighs, stomach, arms, shoulders, and neck. Continue until you tighten your face and relax your face.

End these exercises with breathing in and out slowly.

Week 34: Clothes

Clothing not only covers and protects your body but also provides you an opportunity to be more in tune with the needs of your body. Some people are allergic to some fabrics, like wool, and need to choose their clothing fabrics carefully.

Touch your favorite sweater or any piece of clothing. What do you like about it? This week, wear the clothing that feels the best on your skin.

Week 35: The Walk

Take a walk in nature each day this week. Wherever you live, whether it's the woods, desert, beach, or plains, spend time looking at the trees, flowers, lizards, squirrels, rabbits, any being who crosses your path. Feel the air on your face. Is it cool, windy, warm, moist, or dry? Smell the air during your nature walk. Is there a scent of the season in the air? How would you describe this scent? Listen to the wind move through the trees, bushes, rocks, and notice the sound of any water running. What feelings are evoked during your walk?

Week 36: Almost Exercising

This week you may want to take a break from exercise or limit the amount of strenuous exercise you perform. If you already work out, consider taking a break from the gym and taking a walk. Sometimes shifting your exercise mode to a relaxing state allows your body more recovery time.

If you are considering starting an exercise program, drive to your local gym or place where you have fantasies of working out. Stay in your car and sit there. Don't go into the building. It's not quite time to start working out. But you can start building the habit of going to your local gym or workout studio. Go at a time when you suspect you would like to go to the gym in the future. Go every day this week, and just observe.

If working out is not of any interest to you, consider taking a short 15 minute walk each day this week. Observe how you feel. Did you feel more happy, tired, stressed, or relaxed?

Before you start any workouts, especially if you're tired, see your doctor for a physical.

Week 38: Dancing

This week, dance. Dance when you're at home with your significant other, or dance when you're alone, or dance with your dog, or dance with a friend. Put on some fun music that you enjoy, and move for a few minutes.

How does it feel to move to a rhythm? Do you feel more exhilarated or exhausted? Have you discovered any rhythms or music you had forgotten you liked?

Week 37: Picnics

Go on a picnic by yourself or with your family or friends. Take time in nature to enjoy sitting in a park, eating your favorite picnic food. You can do an entire picnic ritual of packing the food with a tablecloth, spoons, forks, cups, and maybe even grilling food at the park. Or you could buy food to go and sit on a bench as you enjoy observing the outdoors.

How does it feel to you to eat outdoors? Does the food taste different? Do you notice any changes to your appetite? Do you notice any connections with the life around you?

Chapter Seven: Thinking Self-Care

Week 39: Positive Words

In the morning of each day this week, decide on one positive thought, word, or affirmation to think about for the day.

Repeat your thought or word aloud while you're preparing breakfast. You might choose a single word: "Joy."

Or you could choose a sentence: "I feel peaceful now."

During work, every hour on the hour, think of your word or phrase. You could set your watch to chime on the hour.

Write some notes below about any of your observations. Were there situations in which it was easier or more difficult to maintain the thought or phrase? Were there people who helped you to completely forget or remember the positive word or phrase?

Week 40: The Library

This week, visit your public library and sit down inside. Look around you, noticing the stacks of books. What are your favorite types of books? Do you have any memories from your days as a student?

Get a library card and check out one book that interests you. Read it during the week, if you have the energy. Or you could check out an art or travel book and just look at the pictures.

Week 41: Doctors, Dentists, Eye Doctors

To take good care of yourself, it is important to have competent health care professionals who you can rely on to address your health concerns.

This week, jump-start your basic self-care by making appointments for your regular health care visits.

Schedule a visit to your family doctor for your annual physical checkup. If you do not have a family doctor, you may need to screen doctors until you find one you feel comfortable with. Find and schedule a visit to your dentist. Find and schedule a visit to your eye doctor.

You may want to explore other health care modalities, such as acupuncture or chiropractic, in order to enhance your basic self-care.

It is beneficial to have your team of regular health care professionals identified so you are not scrambling to find them in an emergency. You can have peace of mind knowing you are working with people you trust.

Week 42: Humor

When you feel chronically tired, it is difficult to appreciate humor, to laugh, or to even tolerate jokes. However, if there is a movie, TV show, radio show, comic strip, or person who makes you chuckle, seek it out this week.

Take the time each day to appreciate humor, and giggle. You may even find yourself chuckling or laughing out loud.

What types of humor do you enjoy? What types of humor do you dislike?

Week 43: Talk with Your Friend

This week, call a friend you trust with the intention of asking for help with one issue you have. It could be a small issue, such as a referral for a doctor, where to find the best soaps in town, or what movie would help you laugh. Pose a question to your friend.

Bring to the conversation a genuine desire to find a solution. Ask your question, and then wait, breathe, and listen to your friend's questions, comments, or suggestions in response. Take notes. Ask more questions. Listen to the response. When the conversation is over, thank your friend.

Reflect during the week on the conversation. Would this solution work for you? How does the solution feel throughout the week? Check in with yourself if what the person advised makes sense for you. What do you think?

Week 44: Gratitude

Each evening this week, think about one thing you are truly grateful for a few minutes.

If you have the energy, write it down below. It could be something as simple as: my breath; being alive; a warm bed; the moonlight; my friends.

Week 45: Junk Mail

When you receive junk mail this week, notice where it came from and then send it to your recycle bin. Junk mail not only wastes trees used for making paper but also wastes your time sorting and making decisions about the mail itself.

If you see any mail from banks or financial institutions, place that mail on a pile next to your phone. You can stop special offers from your credit card companies, banks, or other financial institutions by calling them and requesting that they stop sending you advertisements, paper checks, or new credit card offers.

You can stop most junk mail by searching on the Internet for "stop junk mail" to find resources to opt out of bulk junk marketing mail.

For example, a nonprofit organization called Forest Ethics works to stop using pristine forests for catalogs at: www.forestethics.org and focuses on stopping bulk junk mail at: www.donotmail.org.

Chapter Eight: Intuiting Self-Care

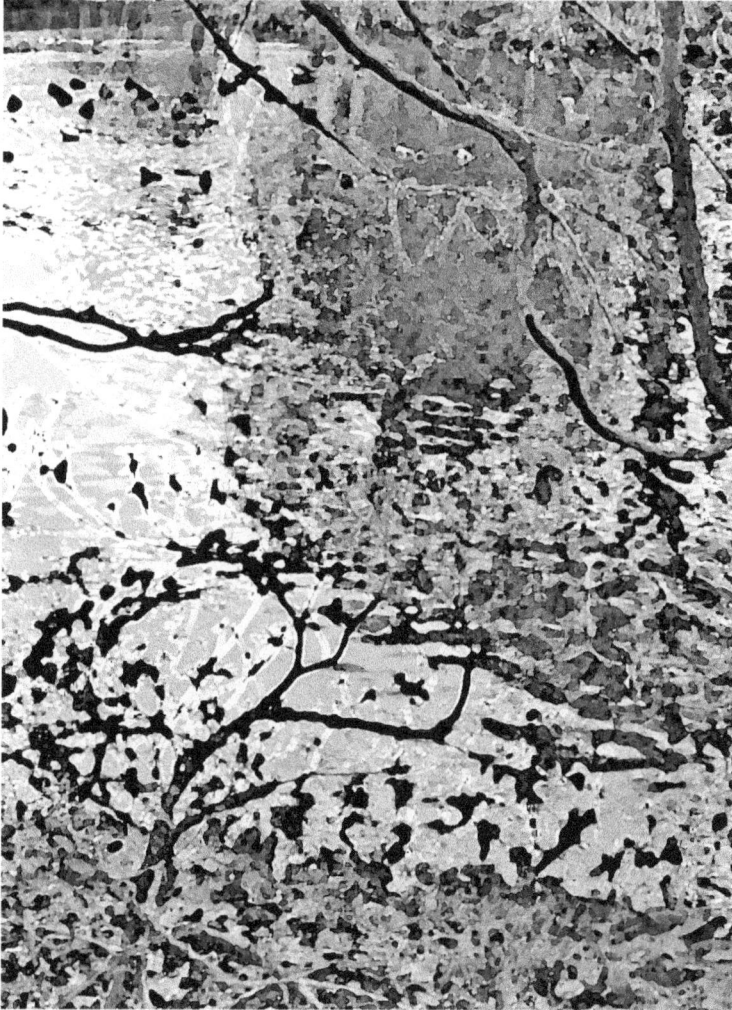

Week 46: Abundance

Redefine abundance. As you look at your gratitude list from previous weeks, notice what you have been grateful for. Many people speak of abundance in terms of financial prosperity. Although this is important, abundance can mean many different things to different people. For example, some people see abundance as having a variety of interesting friends or having the perfect timing in their lives for meeting their life partner, or being joyful daily. Consuming for the sake of consuming does not usually produce the feeling or fact of an abundant life.

This week, explore the question: What does abundance really mean to me? Make some notes below.

Week 47: Doodling

Find a box of crayons, colored pencils, or pens, and doodle. You can doodle while you're in business meetings at work, while you're on the phone at home, while you're sitting quietly. Let your hands move to draw whatever is going through your mind.

Did you notice any insights occurring during the week? Do you notice any themes emerging in what you're thinking about or feeling? Did you notice any themes in your doodling?

Week 48: Light

Being out in the sunlight can lift your feelings. Take the time this week to go on a walk during the daytime in sunlight even if you live in a cooler climate. Notice the light on the trees, animals, or people around you.

With the focus on lighting for energy efficiency, you also might like to consider purchasing full-spectrum lights. Even during the winter months, when the sun does not shine as much, full-spectrum lighting provides you with the light spectrum of the sun.

You might experiment with placing full-spectrum lights in one room in your house. Notice how you feel in that room as compared to how you feel in other rooms. Do you tend to spend more time there? Do you simply feel better? If you notice any positive difference, you may want to consider relighting the rooms in your house or even your office.

Week 49: City, County, State, and National Parks

Take advantage of the free natural resources around you. Is there a local city, county, state, or national park you could visit this week? You don't have to hike or "do" something there.

Simply sitting or walking in a park and enjoying your place in nature can be very soothing. Notice the air, birds, animals, plants, trees, flowers; smell, listen, look, feel the life around you. Receive the rhythm of nature and your place among the living. Let nature nurture you.

What did you receive?

Week 50: Dreams

This week, honestly ask yourself: Is there a dream you feel you've lost? What were the elements of that dream? Is there any one activity of that dream you can reclaim and do?

Make some notes below. Consider doing that one activity of your precious dream.

Week 51: Divine Connecting

This week, consider connecting to the Divine. Regardless of your beliefs or spiritual background, set aside 15 minutes each day to pray, contemplate, or meditate. Any time away from other people, regardless of how you feel, is a good time to step into the Presence. You might experience it as the Presence inside yourself or in nature or in something larger. Experience this Presence as a loving connection.

Did you notice any images, thoughts, or feelings? Did you receive any guidance?

Chapter Nine: Sustaining Self-Care

Week 52: Integrity

This week, look back over the year of small steps. Are there any activities that were especially relevant for you? Are there any pleasures you want to integrate into your life? Are there any activities you would never do again? Perhaps you've become more aware of your preferences.

Are you more aware of your center? How have your choices shifted over this year? Have you noticed your connection with your body, your friends and family, nature around you, and the loving Divine Presence? Did you notice your participation from your center outward into your life?

To sustain any change, incremental steps are best. Is there a small step you have discovered that you would like to continue doing each day to nurture yourself? Make the change with one sustainable, self-care step at a time.

Additional Resources

Dominguez, Joe, and Vicki Robin. *Your Money or Your Life*. London: Penguin Books, 1992.

Keville, Kathi, and Mindy Green. *Aromatherapy: A Complete Guide to the Healing Art*. Freedom, CA: Crossing Press, 1995.

Maclean, Dorothy. *The Call of the Trees*. Everett, WA: Lorian Press, 2006.

Roszak, T., M. Gomes, and A. Kanner, eds. *Ecopsychology: Restoring the Earth, Healing the Mind*. San Francisco: Sierra Club Books, 1995.

Scovel-Shinn, Florence. *Your Word Is Your Wand*. Somerset, UK: C. W. Daniel, 1928.

Website Resources

American Lung Association: www.lungusa.org

Eat Well Guide: www.eatwellguide.org

Forest Ethics: www.forestethics.org

Humane Society of the United States: www.hsus.org

National Park Service: www.nps.gov

NPR Music: www.npr.org/music

Notes

www.ingramcontent.com/pod-product-compliance
Lightning Source LLC
LaVergne TN
LVHW091207080426
835509LV00006B/870